SALES HABITUDE WARRIORS

Sales Strategies that Lead to YES!

Erik Swanson

Habitude Warrior International

Copyright © 2017 Habitude Warrior International -Erik Swanson

All rights reserved.
No part of this publication may be reproduced, stored in a retrieval system, or transmitted, in any form or by any means, without the prior permission in writing of the publisher, nor be otherwise circulated in any form of binding or cover other than that in which it is published and without a similar condition including this condition being imposed on the subsequent purchaser.

Published by Habitude Warrior International
in association with
Elite Online Publishing
Sandy, UT 84070

ISBN-13: 978-1976337116
ISBN-10: 1976337119

DEDICATION

This book is dedicated to one of the best mentors in life I can ever think of... my Mother! What an inspiration to me throughout my life and a fantastic teacher for me to learn the principles of life. Thank you Mom! I love you always!

Your son, Erik

CONTENTS

CHAPTER 1. CREATURES OF HABIT		3
CHAPTER 2. THREE KEYS TO SUCCESS IN SALES		9
CHAPTER 3. GOAL SETTING & GOAL ACHIEVING		15
CHAPTER 4. TIME & EVENT MANAGEMENT		23
CHAPTER 5. PROSPECTING POWER		31
CHAPTER 6. BUILDING A SOURCE OF REFERRALS		37
CHAPTER 7. BUILDING A SOURCE OF TESTIMONIALS		45
CHAPTER 8. BUILDING RAPPORT & CREDIBILITY		49
CHAPTER 9. RECALLING PEOPLE'S NAMES		55
CHAPTER 10. IDENTIFYING PEOPLE'S NEEDS		59
CHAPTER 11. PRESENTATION SKILLS		65
CHAPTER 12. CLOSING & COMMITMENT STRATEGIES		71
CHAPTER 13. OVERCOMING OBJECTIONS		77
CHAPTER 14. SELF-DEVELOPMENT & AWARENESS		81
CHAPTER 15. POSITIVE MENTAL ATTITUDE & SELF TALK		93
BONUS: THE ABUNDANCE THEORY		103

MEET
ERIK SWANSON

Erik Swanson has delivered over 5000 motivational presentations at conferences and meetings worldwide. As a leading award winning Professional Speaker, Best-Selling Author and Attitude Coach, Erik Swanson is in great demand! Speaking on average to more than 50,000 people per year, he is both versatile in his approach and effective in a wide array of training topics.

People call him "**MR. AWESOME**" and you can find him sharing stages with his friends who are some of the most talented and famous speakers and trainers of the world. Erik has shared the stage with Brian Tracy, Les Brown, Jack Canfield, John Assaraf, Sharon Lechter, four-time Olympian Ruben Gonzalez, CEO Space Berny Dohrmann, Millionaire Maker Loral Langemeier, Focus Coach Doug Grady, and even Jim Rohn back in the day.

Erik is a Co-Author of the National Best-Selling book 'Universal Wish' with Greg Scott Reid & Founder of Make a Wish Foundation Frank Shankwitz, and has spoken at Harvard University to their Business and Entrepreneur's School!

What others say About 'Mr. Awesome!

Jeffrey Gitomer, Author of The Little Red Book of Selling, The Sales Bible, and The Little Gold Book of YES! Attitude Pictured Below with Erik "Mr. Awesome" Swanson

"Sales Habitude warriors creates a new awareness for salespeople looking to have a breakthrough and increase their understanding of how sales are made, and turn that awareness into money-making habits. Erik Swanson is Awesome, and his book is powerful - learn to combine attitude and habits into personal profit."

- Jeffrey Gitomer – Best Selling Author/Speaker

"Apply the HABITUDE WARRIOR mindset and watch your habits and relationships change rapidly."

- Brian Tracy - Best Selling Author/Speaker

"Invite Erik to speak to your group. You'll be glad you did!"

- Les Brown - Author/Motivational Speaker

"Mr. Swanson's techniques will not only increase your sales but enhance your careers and lives!"

- Eric Lofholm - International Sales Trainer

"Sales Habitude warriors is the perfect combination for getting next level results. With the right habits and the right attitude sales increase!"

- Bob Donnell - Founder of Everything Next Level

"Allow Erik's principles to change your life!"
- *Greg Scott Reid - Author/Speaker/Filmmaker*

"Erik is a man who captivates attention from the public thanks to his quality of speeches. His kindness and friendship are a treasure to keep forever."
- *Sir 'Chef Bruno' Serato - Owner & Head Chef of The Anaheim White House Restaurant*

"Sales success is an art and science that can be taught and learned. Not only is Erik an excellent sales trainer, but his methods work in the real world with real people right now! Get this book and apply what's inside and watch your sales soar!"
- *John Assaraf - New York Times Best Selling Author "The Answer" and "Having it All"*

"In the journey of success, you come across some amazing people who stand out of the crowd. Erik is one of those people! His books

ARE JAMMED PACKED WITH SALES & LIFE NUGGETS TO INCREASE YOUR INCOME IMMEDIATELY! I HIGHLY RECOMMEND IT. NO WONDER WHY WE ALL CALL HIM "MR. AWESOME"!

- LORAL LANGEMEIER - THE MILLIONAIRE MAKER

"ERIK IS ONE OF THE MOST COMMITTED PEOPLE I KNOW, MAKING A DIFFERENCE IN THE WORLD THROUGH HIS TRAINING MATERIALS AND EVENTS HE PUTS TOGETHER. THIS BOOK IS NO EXCEPTION. HE HAS PUT TOGETHER SOME VERY SIMPLE, YET POWERFUL IDEAS IN AN EASY AND ENJOYABLE FORMAT FOR THE READER."

- DARRYL DAVIS - AUTHOR/PUBLIC SPEAKER/LIFE COACH

"ERIK IS ONE OF THE BEST SPEAKERS I HAVE EVER HEARD! HE'S FUNNY, QUICK-WITTED AND JUST SIMPLY AWESOME! HE WILL MOVE YOUR CROWD."

- DAVID STANLEY - FILMMAKER/PRODUCER/ELVIS PRESSLEY'S BROTHER

"THE SALES & SPEAKER BOOT CAMPS THAT ERIK RUNS IS THE HIGHEST IN THE WORLD IN TURNING OUT 7 FIGURE INCOMES!"

- BERNY DOHRMANN - FOUNDER OF CEO SPACE INTERNATIONAL

MAKE YOUR MEETING A
'SALES HABITUDE WARRIOR' EVENT!
WWW.HABITUDEWARRIOR.COM
TO BOOK INTERNATIONAL SPEAKER AND
BEST-SELLING AUTHOR
ERIK SWANSON
EMAIL US AT
BOOKERIK@HABITUDEWARRIOR.COM

> "YOUR THOUGHTS DETERMINE YOUR ATTITUDE. YOUR ATTITUDE DETERMINES YOUR HABITS. YOUR ***HABITUDES*** DETERMINE YOUR FUTURE!"
>
> *ERIK SWANSON*

Sales Habitude Warriors

CHAPTER 1. CREATURES OF HABIT

Let's face it, we are all creatures of habit! Some habits assist us in life, and some hold us back from our dreams and ambitions. It's time to take control of them, especially if you plan to be super successful in sales. One of the absolute, best gifts you can give yourself is learning how to harness great new habits and making them part of your daily routine. Most people in the world leave their habits and attitudes up to the world to decide instead of taking complete control of them. You have the ability to take that control, yet most people succumb to taking the path of least resistance. Vow today to

NOT be like most people. It's time to change that now! The mark of a highly successful sales pro is one that takes complete control of their future and constantly trains themselves on a daily basis. Just like you wouldn't expect to be in perfect health after hitting the gym only every once in awhile, it's the same principle in becoming a superior sales pro. Let's develop amazing new habits in the areas that follow. But first let's learn how to develop a system of a new habit. Get ready to become a "Habitude Warrior" in Sales!

HOW TO DEVELOP A NEW HABIT

Okay, look, it's super easy to develop a new habit. The hard part is *keeping* that new habit… that's what makes it a 'habit.' Exhaustive studies have told us that a habit is defined by doing something for at least 21 to 30 days in a row. I agree with this, but what I like to teach my clients is to train yourself to do that habit for a minimum of 90 days. Yup, 90 days! That's how you know it's *second nature* to you. So, what are the steps? Here are the 7 steps to developing a new habit:

1. The first step is to decide specifically what your new habit will be. Write it down. Tell Everyone about it. Post it online. Put it on sticky notes everywhere you can in your house, office, car, everywhere! This is called 'Setting up your environment for success."

2. The second step is to write what we call a "30 list." This is a list of 30 passionate reasons why you want to achieve this new habit.

3. Third step is to dig deep and determine what the negative outcomes you will experience by NOT achieving mastery of this new habit.

4. Use what I call the "60 Second Morning Mirror" and have a discussion with yourself every morning for 60 seconds giving yourself praise in advance & telling yourself you are a master at this new habit.

5. Set up mini rewards for each day, week, and month you continually practice the new habit. Only reward yourself when you truly practice the habit daily. Be disciplined with yourself!

6. Set up a completion reward for yourself for completing your new found habit at the end of the

90 days. It doesn't have to be a huge reward, but something that will make you strive for completion of this new habit into second nature for you. Note: Don't reward yourself if you skipped any days during the 90 day focus. If you do skip any days, you literally need to start the 90 days over again.

7. Get Support! Gather for yourself what we call "AP's" or "Accountability Partners." These should NOT be people who are close to you (friends, family.). You need AP's to hold you to the fire when you need their support and be firm and direct with you!

> "A REAL DECISION IS MEASURED BY THE FACT THAT YOU'VE TAKEN A NEW ACTION.
> IF THERE'S NO ACTION, YOU HAVEN'T TRULY DECIDED."
>
> —TONY ROBBINS

Sales Habitude Warriors

CHAPTER 2. THREE KEYS TO SUCCESS IN SALES

There are literally 3 keys to success if you really look at it in becoming a major force in sales in your area; they are *Product Knowledge, Positive Mental Attitude,* and *Sales Strategies.*

Product Knowledge:

It's not only important for you to know the ins and outs of all the divisions of your product or service, but you also need to know about your competitor's products as well. In addition, you definitely need to know what your prospect's situation is and what their past was in regard to any product or service that's similar to yours. Why did they choose it? Why did they not choose it? Which feature did they appreciate the most? Ask them this: "Were you *completely satisfied* with XYZ?" "What would you have changed if you could have?" Get them talking and giving you answers along the way! But, let me ask you a question. Have you ever met someone who has excellent product or service knowledge, yet they couldn't convey or communicate it over to their prospect? Maybe they were negative in the business…

This brings me to the next Key you need to possess…

Positive Mental Attitude:

How many of you know someone with an 'NMA' which stands for a Negative Mental Attitude! You must make a habit of maintaining a really great attitude during each and every day, especially in sales. Let's face it, if you're in sales, you're going to get beaten up a lot out there. And if you're not, maybe you're not hitting as much prospecting and doors or calls as you need to each day. Like one of my mentors used to tell me, you need to act like a duck in the rain when you're out there in sales and simply allow the rejection and objections slide off your back like the rain water off a duck's back. Make sense? Stop taking things so personally! When someone says 'no' to you, they are saying 'no' to themselves, not to YOU! Got it?!

It's so funny when I meet so many people who love to deal with all the negatives in the world instead of the positives. I mean, I meet some people who even have positive things that happen to them, yet they find a negative spin on it. "You just won a million dollars!" … and they say "Yeah, but taxes!" Resolve and vow never to be like that! Have reminders if you need to. I wear a bracelet every day which says "Remember to PEA! - Be Positive, Energetic & AWESOME today!!!

Number 3 is a Quick Key to Sales Success is…

Sales Strategies:

This is literally the nuts and bolts of the sales process from meeting the prospect, building instant and long lasting rapport and credibility, and taking them all the way to them saying YES to you and your product or service. It's what we say, how we say it, and when we say it. It's also a series of what we *don't* say that will assist us in this process. Have you ever said something to a prospect and you wish you could have taken it right back? Well, in the chapters to follow, we will share with you great techniques to start utilizing right away to make more sales and bring your productivity up in a major way! Your competition will be jealous and of your success and want to know what your trick is. Just smile at them and say 'Huh, I must be *Lucky'!* Isn't it funny how the graph of success for any highly successful person usually reads like this: Failure, failure, failure, failure, failure, failure, failure, failure, failure, failure... **_WILD SUCCESS!_** Then people start pointing at you and saying "Wow, he or she was just lucky!" Well, let's make that happen and let's make you *'Lucky'* then. Maybe we should have named the book by that title. Just kidding. Okay, let's get started!

> "Setting goals is the first step in turning the invisible into the visible."
>
> —Tony Robbins

Sales Habitude Warriors

CHAPTER 3. GOAL SETTING & GOAL ACHIEVING

"SUCCESS IS GOALS, AND EVERYTHING ELSE IS COMMENTARY" ~ BRIAN TRACY

Goal Setting & Goal Achieving:

Goal setting is vital to any sales organization and every sales pro! It's a benchmark to strive for on a consistent basis and allows you to raise your own bar of excellence. The highly successful Habitude Warrior Sales Pro won't wait until their manager sets their goals for them… but in fact, they will set higher and higher goals to strive for personal excellence. To be a 'Habitude Warrior' means to not only go the extra mile but to run at full speed without fear for that extra 100 miles! It's becoming ***Unstoppable*** in the pursuit of excellence. Who better to commit to than yourself? In fact, while learning and having the pleasure of sharing the stage with Jim Rohn years ago in Houston, he reminds us to always work harder on yourself than anything else…, and everything will start to flourish around you in your life. It's magical!

Goal Setting:

Most people in the world, sadly, do not have any real direction in their lives and a very small percentage of them actually have a working list of written goals. Studies have told us year after year that only about 3% to 5% of sales people actually have written goals. That's crazy! You absolutely need to commit and resolve to yourself to join the top 3% of Habitude Warriors. It's very simple to do… but, the flip side of that is it's also very simply ***not*** to do either.

When I started in the industry as a National Sales Trainer back in 1997, we had the pleasure to work with many different types of industries to train their sales teams. One of those industries was the sports industry in which we assisted not only the corporate sales and advertising teams, but also assisted in attitude training for the actual athletes. One of the coolest things we had found out while working in the Chicago area one year was the fact that Michael Jordan had been writing down his goals since he was 5 years old! FIVE YEARS OLD! Wow, that's powerful. Do you think we can learn from successful people? Absolutely! It's called 'modeling.' Do you think we can learn from unsuccessful people? Sure! Simply do what they are not doing and learn the correct adjustments for success.

When Dr. Napoleon Hill wrote the world famous book 'Think and Grow Rich,' he followed around and studied more than 500 highly successful business people to see which traits they had in common and which traits they didn't have in common. Guess what, goals and having a definiteness of purpose was one of the top traits he found in common. Success leaves clues. The problem with most individuals is that they want to try and reinvent the wheel when all they really need to do is 'model' and do what has worked for millions of individuals before them; almost like a recipe to follow when cooking. If you plan to get the same result in that recipe, you simply need to follow the ingredients and the timing to the tee. Don't forget, your goals need to be as specific as possible! Let me share with you *my* goal setting technique:

7 TIPS TO SETTING CLEAR & CONCISE GOALS

Step 1: Make an absolute decision for success in your specific goal & vow to commit to do whatever it takes to reach this goal.

Step 2: Write the goal in the present tense as if already accomplished.

Step 3: Write the goal down in as many places as possible so you can see it each and every day. (At work, at home, on car visor, etc.)

Step 4: Set up a 'Win Date' (or deadline) for completion of your goal.

Step 5: Tell all of your family, friends, & colleagues about your goal.

Step 6: Write down 3 new reasons each day why you want to achieve it!

Step 7: Review your goal every evening and every morning for 10 min.

What's the difference between Goal Setting vs. Goal Achieving? Well, setting goals are fantastic and absolutely necessary, but that's not all you have to do. There are specific ways to make sure you ***achieve*** those particular goals as well. Here are some tips to help you with that:

7 TIPS TO ACHIEVING CLEAR & CONCISE GOALS

Step 1: Visualize yourself already in a successful state with your goal.

Step 2: Download photos and make a 'vision board' to reflect your goal.

Step 3: Use the 'PME' technique which stands for 'Positive Mental Environment' & set up your environment for your goal's success.

Step 4: Every day, 10 times each hour, tell yourself in present tense this statement and add in your goal to the sentence: **"I am ………."**

Step 5: Set up an amazing reward for yourself when you achieve the goal.

Step 6: Repeat these words out loud every single day in the mirror in the morning for 60 seconds: "I am the best; I am the best; I am the best; I can do this! I can do this! I can achieve this! I am this! This is mine! (and make sure you personalize it to your goal)

Step 7: Get an AP which is an Accountability Partner or Coach to report to each day on your success towards reaching your goal.

> "IN THE MIDST OF MOVEMENT AND CHAOS, KEEP STILLNESS INSIDE OF YOU."
> —DEEPAK CHOPRA

Sales Habitude Warriors

CHAPTER 4. TIME & EVENT MANAGEMENT

Time management is notorious for being the number two reason, statistically why salespeople are not as successful as they would like to be. Can you guess what the number one reason that stands in a salesperson's way is—It's **Fear**! You know, the fear of failure; the fear of ridicule; the fear of trying the unknown; even the fear of success. Fear really is just a state of mind in which you can easily transform it to assist you in harvesting great new habits! But let's get back to 'time management.' Could you use an extra two or three hours per day?

Do you sometimes feel you have too much month at the end of the money? Do you always feel like you need a vacation? Or worse, do you need a vacation from your vacation? Well, you're not alone. A ton of salespeople have this issue and it holds them back from the wild success that is simply waiting for them. The problem with most individuals is that they try to get everything done all at once, and they get in their own way. They want everything to be perfect, and they stress out that they are not getting the important things done in their lives. That's the "Habitude Warrior's" definition of 'Stress.' Stress is when you are not accomplishing the goals you have set out for yourself in the time perimeters you have allotted. It's tough, we know. I absolutely agree that this area is a killer in most sales careers. But we are here to help! Here are some tips below to start implementing ***immediately;*** that's the key when it comes to time management.

Habit Tip 1: Act Immediately!

Don't delay! Use the Habitude Warrior "**Platinum Law of 48**" which simply says to act upon an idea and put your wheels in motion within a measure of 48! If it's a smaller idea or task act within *48* *minutes*. If it's a business building idea, then *48 hours* applies. Even if it's a personal goal or idea, act right away and do something, anything, towards the realization of that particular idea. Chances are if you do not implement the idea at hand within that time period then it will simply be wasted. This is where procrastination comes into play. The simple way to beat procrastination is to use these 3 simple but powerful words and say to yourself: ***DO IT NOW!***

Habit Tip 2: Time Block (Event Management)

Use the time blocking theory in which you literally block out certain times of the day and workweek to complete certain tasks… such as blocking out 2 hours per day to answer emails. Personally, I block out 45 minutes in the morning, and 45 minutes in the afternoon. I also set up my email signature to let people know the times in which I return all email replies. This is super important to teach and train others how you would like to be treated. You need to let them know that they are not in control of your life and your time and that you control it! Just like when we were little kids, we would have to let others know how we wanted to be treated on the playground. It's the same concept here. I use the same theory with my voicemail at work and mobile phone. Let people know when you plan to return all calls. They will respect you more for this technique. Finally, Event Management; let's all agree that we **cannot** literally manage time, but we can manage our events and our actions we take during each and every day. A good friend of mine, and great Speaker and Author, Terry Gogna, who resides in the Toronto area calls this 'PEM' standing for 'Priority Event Management'… which leads me to my next Habit Tip.

Habit Tip 3: Prioritize Your Day!

Start the night before. This is huge! Take at least 10 minutes at the end of your day to prioritize a list for you to accomplish the very next day. I can't tell you how important this tip is, yet, most people simply don't do it. It's very easy to do… and very easy not to do. You will be astonished at your success results once you implement this idea (Remember, use the Platinum Law of 48 and implement it within the next 48 hours). Find a system and use it consistently. I use a spiral notepad for my daily prioritization. You can use your computer, tablet or smartphone instead if that works best for you. The point is to use one system and stick with it. Another point is to make sure this system you're using will be in front of you constantly at the end of the day and the beginning of the day. This is called **'TOMA'** which stands for Top Of Mind Awareness. At the end of each day write down 10 to 20 tasks or items you need to get accomplished the next day. Place the letter 'A' next to the tasks with the highest importance and **A**bsolutely needs to get done. Place a 'B' next to the tasks that can take a **B**ackseat until the afternoon. Place a 'C' next to the tasks that can be **C**ontinued over to the next day. Place a 'D' next to the tasks that can be **D**elegated to someone else (as in your assistant or outsource it). Finally, place an 'E' next to the tasks that you can actually **E**liminate out of your day completely and do not even need to be on your list. These last 2 are very liberating. It's a great feeling to know that you simply will never get everything done, nor do you need to. Practice 'Selective Procrastination' in which you procrastinate on items that simply don't hold a value in their accomplishment. The way you can tell this is by asking yourself this golden question: Does this task I'm about to work on have a direct & positive impact in the accomplishment of one of my major definite goals? If it doesn't, then eliminate it all-together!

BONUS HABIT TIP: "DOUBLE DOUBLE"

I wanted to share a bonus tip for you that I'm positive you will love. It's called "Double Double" which is a Habitude Warrior commitment to myself in which I am committing to doubling my income from last year to this year; and at the same time, I will double the time off that I do it in. Pretty cool Habitude, don't you think? And what if I fail by 20%, 30% or even 50%… I'm still way ahead of the game! Challenge: Put this technique into action and commit to yourself to do something, anything over the next 48 hours in implementing a new idea for growth.

> "HOW PEOPLE TREAT YOU IS THEIR KARMA; HOW YOU REACT IS YOURS."
>
> -WAYNE DYER

Sales Habitude Warriors

CHAPTER 5. PROSPECTING POWER

The true "Habitude Warrior" knows that prospecting is never out for the true sales pro! There are smart ways to prospect and gather new clients. The rule of thumb is to always use the 80/20 rule in which you prospect 80% of the time and you present and follow up 20% of the time with existing clients. Don't switch them and get this wrong! I teach and coach my team to prospect in many different ways. Here are a few tips:

Habit Tip 1: Use the Clover Technique

If you have an appointment at 11 am at XYZ company, go early and hit 3 doors up, 3 doors down, and 6 doors across. This will generate 12 self-generated leads for yourself, **and** you can use the 11 am appointment as somewhat of a referral. Your point in hitting these doors is to simply drop in and shake their hand and maybe drop off some quick information or gift for them (like this book!). Make sure you let them know you are busy and have to run because you are working with XYZ company down the street or hallway. This gives instant credibility.

Habit Tip 2: Twelve Business Cards Per Day

I always leave my homes or hotel when traveling with at least 12 business cards in my wallet every single day. This is a habit now. Do it. It works. I commit to myself to pass at least 12 business cards out per day. Sometimes I challenge myself and pass the 12 business cards out by noon. This means I have to meet 12 new business contacts before I can finish my actual day of work as a sales professional. This technique alone can change your sales career in a major way. Your goal is to get 12 business cards back from your new contacts that you have just met.

Habit Tip 3: Seven Social Media Contacts Per Day

Each day I make a point to connect with at least 7 contacts through any means of social media. It only takes about 10 to 20 minutes per day to do this technique, but, wow, what a difference in results! Now, there are some rules to this technique. Don't, and I'll repeat, **DON'T** just send out the same 'copy and paste' email to 7 different contacts daily. You have to customize the email to them and introduce yourself quickly, but more importantly, ask them how you can assist them in growing **their** business. This is huge and really gets amazing results in reply. The more you assist others to get what they want, the more the universe starts to deliver what you want. It's the most amazing thing!

Sales Habitude Warriors

> "Expect the best.
> Prepare for the worst.
> Capitalize on what comes."
>
> -Zig Ziglar

Sales Habitude Warriors

CHAPTER 6. BUILDING A SOURCE OF REFERRALS

Building referrals are easy to do once you learn the secret to doing it. Do you know what the #1 reason why people don't actually get referrals in their business? I'm sure you guessed it; they simply don't ask! That's why this is a very important Habitude to conquer and keep through your career in sales. Build this habit early and often, and you will see a huge value it has in growing your business. The second reason why people don't gather that many referrals in their business is simply because they don't know the proper way to ask for them. I'm here to help!

Mentality of Referrals

You first need to build a strong and positive mentality of referrals. When I first started out as a trainer for Brian Tracy years ago, for the first few years I didn't see the value of gathering referrals. I was under what they call 'Unconscious - Incompetent" at the time. I *didn't know* what I *didn't know*. Sounds funny, right? But it's true. I was SO busy worrying about just 'getting the sale' that I didn't put much effort or thought into gathering referrals for my long-term success. I was too deep in the forest to see the trees around me, so to say. Then, a trigger when off in my mind. I started to see a pattern as I traveled back to the same cities that I had previously done business in. I started running into the same clients, yet they were at different companies or associations, and now they were actually in Management! Perfect! They welcomed me in with open arms to their new company or association. See, my reputation followed *ME* rather than just my company or job. They were welcoming *ME* into their new establishment. And they were very happy to refer me to others as well. All I had to do is ***ASK***... so that's exactly what I started to do. I soon realized that by me asking for referrals from everyone I come across, I was actually helping and enhancing people's lives and company's production because I believe in myself, my product, and of course my company! I also have a proven track record. If you don't ask, you certainly won't get. Wayne Gretzky said it best when he said; "You miss 100% of the shots you don't take!"

Here are some quick *Habitudisms* I would say to myself to pump myself up to ask for referrals: *"I am worth it! I am worth a source of referrals. I deserve to gather referrals. People love to refer me to others. I help so many people grow in their business and lives. I am definitely worth it!"*

How to Properly Ask for Referrals:

There are so many ways people try to ask for referrals... and so many of them are dead wrong. That's the problem. People tend to try asking, and it doesn't work, so then they just simply don't ask anymore. Here's the best way we have found to ask for a referral. But wait, before I tell you what that is… let me ask you a question: Can you ask for referrals from people who are not your clients yet? Answer: of course! It's a funny thing, but as long as you are professional, nice, courteous, and the person likes and trusts you, then even if they are not a client of yours, they will still be more than happy to refer you to someone who may be a better fit to utilize you and your services. So, our mantra is:

Ask Everyone; Ask Often; & Ask Everyone!

Best Way to Ask:

"By the way, I was just thinking about something. I wouldn't be doing my job if I didn't ask you for some referrals. From what I've gathered and seen, you are such a progressive thinker and leader in your industry; I'm sure you know a lot of people we might be able to work with as well and bring a ton of value to their company. I would absolutely love it if you would be so kind as to be able to introduce me to some other companies you feel would benefit from what we do. Here's what I'm actually looking for… I'm looking for (**Note: be as specific as you can be when asking for this next part**) companies in this area (name the city or geographic area you're in or looking for clients in. Don't be so broad here. Be specific and clear!) who have at least 10 to 15 sales professionals on their team. Can you think of another manager of one of those companies or associations that you know pretty well who you wouldn't mind introducing me to?" They say, "SURE." You say: "Great! In fact, think you can give them a call right now while I'm here and introduce me to them over the phone? And even if you get their voicemail, we can leave a quick message." This works so well when you simply ask! It's amazing how many people would like to assist others, and the main reason why they don't is simply because they were never asked. The way I figure, strike while the iron is hot… so ask them to call them right away. It's fresh in their minds and you will see magic happen right before your eyes. Now, keep in mind, your job is NOT to 'sell' the referral on your products or services yet. Your job is to simply introduce yourself, wet their appetites on you and what you could potentially offer them, use the testimonial of who just referred you, and 'step sell' this into an appointment to meet. That's it. Done.

> "A GOAL IS A DREAM WITH A DEADLINE."
>
> -NAPOLEON HILL

Sales Habitude Warriors

CHAPTER 7. BUILDING A SOURCE OF TESTIMONIALS

It's vitally important to realize that it doesn't matter what you say as much as it matters what *others* say about you! Let's face it, word of mouth travels super-fast these days. You need to capture this trend and utilize it in your Habitude Sales Process. Get really, really good at gathering testimonials and watch your business skyrocket! Statistics tell us that one letter of testimony is worth at least one hour of a presentation in front of a prospect. Wow, that's huge. But, guess what... a *Video Testimonial* is worth even more. Set a Habitude Goal to gather at least 3 testimonials from existing clients per week for the next year. You will have at least 150 testimonials by the end of the year. Put all of these testimonials on your YouTube Channel! If you don't have one yet, go get one. It's free. Come on… Get one in the next 48 minutes! OK?!

Best Way to Ask for Testimonials:
"How can I get that in writing, OR better yet, let's do a quick 30-second video where we can highlight you first, and then highlight me!"

> "Think continually about what you want, not about the things you fear."
>
> –Brian Tracy

Sales Habitude Warriors

CHAPTER 8. BUILDING RAPPORT & CREDIBILITY

Studies tell us that everything counts when building up rapport, credibility and ultimately building up a long-lasting client relationship.

Appearance Counts:

The way you present yourself says a lot as a first impression. The golden rule is to always leave your house in the morning looking like one of the top 5% of your industry. People want to work with people who are organized and focused, not disorganized and out of sorts. This also applies to your vehicle as well. Make sure you look sharp at all times. Another great rule to remember is that it's always easier to dress down rather than dressing backup. Dress to impress.

Smile for Success:

Make sure you throw a smile as many times as you can per day. The great thing about a smile is that it transcends any language in any country. It makes the world go around in a major positive way.

Eye Contact:

Great eye contact builds trust. They say having great eye contact for about 3 or 4 seconds is perfect. Anything over that is considered 'stalking!' (Just kidding; sort of!)

Firm Handshake:

Having a firm handshake goes a long way to share your confidence in yourself as well as your product and service. But not too firm though. I had met someone one time who was wearing one of those huge graduation rings who shook my hand so hard that once I took my hand away from him, I looked at my hand and I could see the imprint of when he graduated school. That's too hard!

Use the 90/10 Rule:

Everyone has heard about the '80/20 Rule'… well, I recommend you use my '90/10 Rule' to build fantastic relationships. The rule is simple. All you have to do is spend about 90% of the time talking about 'them' and only 10% of the time talking about 'you.' Show them that you truly care about who they are and what they stand for, rather than talking about ourselves way too much. People love to be heard and truly understood. So vow to spend 90% of the time learning about them.

Sales Habitude Warriors

> "Learn how to be happy with what you have while you pursue all that you want."
>
> -Jim Rohn

Sales Habitude Warriors

CHAPTER 9. RECALLING PEOPLE'S NAMES

Everyone's favorite word is their own name. Yet, so many people simply don't train themselves to recall people's names. Instead, they say to themselves; "Now, don't forget their name!" I'd rather you change that to saying to yourself "You know, I'm REALLY great at recalling people's names!" It's simply getting your subconscious mind into congruency with your conscious mind to be excellent at this Sales Habitude. After I had taken many memory training courses which seemed to only confuse me more, I decided to develop my own system. I called it "***Bracketing***." My record utilizing this system is now recalling 158 names in one meeting. Not bad, huh? It was AWESOME!

Bracketing Technique to Name Recalling:

1. Place their name at the beginning of your first sentence
2. Place their name at the end of your next sentence
3. Repeat their name 3 to 5 times. **NOT OUT LOUD !!!**

"Don't join an easy crowd; you won't grow.

Go where the expectations and the demands to perform are high."

-Jim Rohn

Sales Habitude Warriors

CHAPTER 10. IDENTIFYING PEOPLE'S NEEDS

In order to turn a prospect into becoming one of your clients, it's important to identify their true needs before offering any of your products or services. The best way to find this out is to ask them great, qualifying questions. We use the acronym "NEEDS."

N: Now

Find out where they are 'now.' This will give you clues. It's almost like this... if I were lost and called you for directions, your first question to me would be "where are you now?"

E: Enjoy
What does your prospect 'enjoy' about the current product or service they already have? Find out why they love it. Or, if they love it. Get some great buzzwords here from their answers that you will actually use later in your closing sequences.

E: Environment
What is the actual 'environment' they are seeking? Give them examples. Paint a picture of the ideal environment that a lot of your existing clients rave about while utilizing your products or services.

D: Decision Makers
Who was in the decision-making process of their exciting product or service? Here's the best way we have found to ask: "Besides yourself of course, was there anyone else who assisted you in making the decision to use XYZ?"

S: Solutions
Finally, based on the above information and intel you just received, it's time for you to present your

'solution' to fill their true 'need.' It's super important to make sure your solution fits their true need. Otherwise, you still may make the sale, but you won't gain a long lasting relationship.

It's also important to realize that sometimes you won't be the actual solution for every prospect. In these cases, the classy thing to do and a sign of the true Sales Habitude Warrior is for you to refer your prospect to a competitor who you believe actually does have their solution.

Sales Habitude Warriors

> "Formal education will make you a living; self-education will make you a fortune."
>
> - Jim Rohn

CHAPTER 11. PRESENTATION SKILLS

Your presentation is where you can really shine! Each of your presentations needs attention to detail no matter how small, or large your audience is. When I speak to groups of 5, 500, or 5000, I always remind myself that it's very important to treat each group with a ton of respect no matter what. In the sales process, your presentation is where you make your case for them to choose you over any of your competition. Remember that your presentation needs to focus and answer the direct questions you feel your prospects have in their minds to be able to make a clear choice in deciding to work with you and your company. Prospects have so many choices these days. Let's face it, there is so much competition out there. We need to stand out from your competitors. Remember to use the acronym "WIIFM" which stands for *"What's In It For Me?"* This is what your prospects are always thinking when you present to them. What will they get from utilizing YOU!

Present the Best Solution

Here is a formula we use to present a great solution. This is so vital to any presentation or conversation. Schools should make this Habitude a must for every student.

Here is a 7 key checklist you must have:

1) Product Knowledge! Knowledge of your product & service is key to a great presentation. Know your competition's as well!

2) Know your audience! Do your homework and find out more about your prospects, and what makes them buzz.

3) Know your timing! If your prospect agrees to see you for 15 minutes, then only take 13 minutes of their time.

4) Use Testimonials! A great thing to sprinkle into your presentation are testimonials from other very happy clients.

5) Get them to participate! Ask questions you already know that your prospect could agree "YES" to.

6) Give Examples! Give your prospect examples of the benefits of other happy clients in similar businesses as your prospect.

7) Have fun! Be yourself and be comfortable. It will show!

Sales Habitude Warriors

> "Motivation is what gets you started. Habit is what keeps you going."
>
> -Jim Rohn

Sales Habitude Warriors

CHAPTER 12. CLOSING & COMMITMENT STRATEGIES

The best closing techniques are obviously the ones that don't even seem like they are closing techniques. Do you know the #1 reason why people don't get 'the close?' It's because we never ask the prospect to buy. Studies tell us the prospect would have bought had the salesperson simply asked the prospect to buy. But, we simply don't ask. Why don't we ask? The answer most of the time is because of a 4 letter word called "FEAR!" Here's a tip: fear is typically only in the mind of the beholder. And another thing to remember is that 80% of the things we worry about typically never happen. And the other 20% we have no control over anyway. So, don't allow "Fear" to get in your way of asking for the order, or asking for those referrals, or testimonials. You are worth it, and you owe it to your prospect to ask them to take advantage of your product or service because you truly believe in your product or service!

Here are 2 fantastic Closing Strategies:

1) "It makes sense to me, wouldn't you agree?"

After giving a great presentation to your prospect and of course after identifying their need, simply turn to them and ask them this amazing question: It makes sense to me, wouldn't you agree? And then simply be quiet. Let them respond. They can only have two possible choices of responses... either "Yes" or "No." Keep in mind that a "Maybe" is still a "No." So, if they say YES, then you congratulate them on making a great choice and let them know you are going to take care of all of the details. Your customer always wants to know that you are there for them every step of the way. Otherwise, they could have purchased your product or service on their own. You can use what is called a "Peripheral Close" right then by asking them how they would like to pay for the product or service. It's brilliant. If you give them an alternative method of payments and they choose one of them, then they are actually choosing "YES" to your product or service in the first place. Peripheral and Alternative closes are great ways to direct the attention towards an easy item to say yes to and lessen any pressure.

2) "We are not trying to be the low-cost provider. We are the low-risk provider!"

This is a great way to close on price and handle any cost objections at the same time. Let's admit it that we all meet those prospects who want *ALL* of our services; *ALL* of our time; *ALL* of our efforts … yet, how much do they want to pay for that… *Nothing!* So, let's change that by using this closing sequence. "We are not *trying* to be the low cost provider. This implies that others are cutting their costs and we all know you get what you pay for. We *are* the low *risk* provider! No one wants to take a big risk, especially in this investment in your (fill it in with your product or service) home, in your family, in your future, etc." See how that works? They will completely agree with you… and if you're doing it correctly by using the 'mirror and matching' technique and nodding your head yes while speaking to them…they will nod their head as well and say something like "you're right, yes." Boom! The sale is completed… Now all you have to do is go to that first close that I shared with you and simply say to them something like "Great, it makes sense to me, wouldn't you agree then?" They say "yes." You say "Perfect; Congratulations. I will take care of all of the details then. You are in great hands working with me!"

> "LIFE HAS NO LIMITATIONS, EXCEPT THE ONES YOU MAKE."
>
> -LES BROWN

Sales Habitude Warriors

CHAPTER 13. OVERCOMING OBJECTIONS

Overcoming & Handling Objections is just the name of the game. You absolutely need to get GREAT at it! It's where a ton of sales people lose their momentum and ultimately lose the deal.

Here are 5 steps to handling an objection of any kind:

1) Acknowledge them and their objection and compliment them. *(Actually, compliment them for bringing it up to your attention)*

2) Pause and Use their Name (*Using their name and pausing makes them feel more comfortable*)

3) Rephrase and Question the Objection (*Literally recite the question back to them by rephrasing it*)

4) S-H-U-T-U-P (*Actually be super quiet here and allow them to speak*)

5) Answer It (*Give them a concise and accurate answer explaining how and why the value of the product or service far outweighs the price*)

"Life takes on meaning when you become motivated, set goals and charge after them in an unstoppable manner."

-Les Brown

Sales Habitude Warriors

CHAPTER 14. SELF-DEVELOPMENT & AWARENESS

Developing yourself is one of the most important Habitudes you can have in your life and will benefit not only in your sales career but also in your personal life! When I spoke on stage with the late & great philosopher, Jim Rohn, he used to tell us to work harder on ourselves than our jobs and not only will our careers grow but all areas of our lives will be improved. When I worked with Brian Tracy for years, he used to tell us to use the 1% formula and vow to get better simply 1% every day in a certain area of our lives. It truly works! I borrowed a fantastic tip and made it one of my Secret Habitudes (Do you have my other book yet... "Secret

Habitudes") from a great friend of mine, amazing Speaker and four-time Olympian, Ruben Gonzalez, who explained to me that he reads 3 books a month! He reads one book on his chosen field/career. His second book he reads is on how to constantly become a better parent. His third book is on something he has no knowledge about yet. Awesome, isn't it? I have adapted this Habitude. You should too!

There are so many ways to improve yourself and do what I call "Leveling Up." The rule of thumb back in the day when I started in sales was what they called "Rule of Three." It was suggested to read 3 books a year in sales. Study 3 CDs (or back in the day it used to be cassettes!) courses a year. Attend 3 live seminars a year. The Rule of Three has changed slightly over the years for me. I would only suggest that Rule of Three outlined above for beginners in sales. I truly believe it's simply not enough. We need to immerse ourselves with all of the fantastic trainers and teachers of our day. You owe it to yourself, to your family, and also to your prospects! Here's what I do… I read 3 books a month. I am constantly taking at least 3 training courses a month, whether it's online or CDs or DVDs or webinars, etc. And, I attend at least 3 seminars each quarter… so at least 12 seminars a year. This strategy will help you tremendously. The more training you have, they more ammunition you have to enter into the battle of sales. The way I figure, it's better to have more choices than less. Arm yourself with great leaders, trainers, and speakers. Search them out. Ask people to refer you to their mentors and trainers. And then immerse yourself. Learn from the best in your industry!

Self-Development Assessment

It's very important to take an evaluation of your own self development to see where you are and what areas you need to improve on. Our coaching clients evaluate themselves each quarter to stay sharp and keep that competitive edge.

Evaluate & Rate Yourself In Each Area Below:
(1 is super low, 5 average and 10 being an expert)

Goal Setting Techniques   1 2 3 4 5 6 7 8 9 10

Time Management Skills   1 2 3 4 5 6 7 8 9 10

Prospecting Techniques   1 2 3 4 5 6 7 8 9 10

Referral Gathering Skills   1 2 3 4 5 6 7 8 9 10

Building Up Credibility   1 2 3 4 5 6 7 8 9 10

Recalling People's Names   1 2 3 4 5 6 7 8 9 10

Identifying People's Needs   1 2 3 4 5 6 7 8 9 10

Presenting Solutions   1 2 3 4 5 6 7 8 9 10

Closing Strategies   1 2 3 4 5 6 7 8 9 10

Overcoming Objections   1 2 3 4 5 6 7 8 9 10

Positive Mental Attitude   1 2 3 4 5 6 7 8 9 10

Self-Development Assessment FOLLOW UP

How did you do in the self-evaluation? A great idea to do now would be to ask someone you trust to evaluate yourself as well in those areas. Ask a colleague or even a superior in your business. Get a real sense of where you are and which areas you need the most improvement in. Our study tells us that each point in each area costs us income. If your income in sales is about $100,000, then each point in each area costs you about $10,000 per year. If you are just starting out and you're around the $50,000 to $60,000 income range, then each point in each area costs about $5000 to $6000 a year. You get the point. Now, add them all up. You'll soon see that simply by raising a point in each of those main critical factor areas of sales you can raise your income by thousands and thousands of dollars. In the example of being around the $100k income range, simply improving 1 point in each area would yield an income increase of another $110,000 a year! That literally DOUBLES your income by this simple technique of the Self-Development Assessment System.

*** Would you like more assistance in your growth? ***

Check out this website for FREE training videos and audios!

www.HabitudeWarrior.com

AWARENESS

How aware are you of your surroundings? Most people have what we call 'blinders' on in sales. They walk around thinking they know what they are looking for and they are so intense in finding it that they miss the all-important surroundings. There are so many opportunities all around us every single day. You just have to be open to accepting these opportunities and open up your awareness to them. A fantastic book was written by the Best Selling Author, Eckhart Tolle. The name of the book is ***"Power of Now."*** Pick up this book, read it, absorb it, and practice its principles. What a great read.

What I like to do to be proactive and practice my "Awareness," is to use this Sales Habitude that you should implement immediately. It's called, **"Take a Different Route."**

This technique will allow you to open your awareness of things you haven't noticed before. It also gets you out of the regular occurrences you typically surround yourself with each day. Here's what you do. Each week you pick a day to take a different route to get to a certain place you're supposed to go to. Don't take the regular path or route or highway. In fact, get off of the highway and take side roads as much as you can. This will open your eyes to so many more opportunities… and if you're in sales, that's what we are looking for. You want to meet as many people as you possibly can if you're in sales. It's not what you know, it's who you know. Or, better yet, it's who knows YOU!

Another idea I implement is the fact that I never fill up my gas tank to full. I always fill it up about 1/2 way. This means I'm at a gas station twice as many times are you are. Let me ask you a question. Do you have a butler? No, I didn't think so. So, that means you most likely pump your own gas at gas stations, correct? Well, that's perfect… that means I have a chance to meet you while I'm pumping my gas across the pumps from you. I'll just strike up a quick and nice conversation and comment on something I can genuinely give you a compliment on such as "Nice car!"

Search out opportunities of networking groups and mixers. Don't
keep going to the same ones all of the time. Search new ones in your area. Or better yet, get out of *your*

area and drive to different ones in different surrounding areas. Meet different people. Open up your awareness. I even book a flight somewhere for no reason! It works.

Sales Habitude Warriors

"Life is a gift, and it offers us the privilege, opportunity, and responsibility to give something back by becoming more."

-Tony Robbins

Sales Habitude Warriors

CHAPTER 15. POSITIVE MENTAL ATTITUDE & SELF TALK

How would you rate yourself on a scale of 1 to 10 in your ability to stay positive throughout your day? Are you in charge of your attitude or do you allow others to determine your attitude for you? Are you allowing others to *rent* space in your mind and you're not even charging them rent for it! Ultimately, if you allow others to determine your attitude, then you also allow them to determine your outcome and your future. Suggestion: ***Don't allow them to do this!***

Pump Yourself Up
I recommend you use this Sales Habitude of "Pumping Yourself Up" each day and throughout

your day. Things are going to happen. They are just things happening. They hold no meaning until you actually place a meaning to them, or worse you allow others to place that meaning to them for you. I would like you to develop a CREED that you say to yourself each morning and during certain times of the day.

My creed includes about 10 statements that I pump myself up with each morning and strategically throughout the day. I place my creed in different areas where I will be. For example, I'll place a copy of my creed on my refrigerator. Another one will be on my bathroom mirror. Another one in front of the coffee maker. Another one in my car on my visor. Another one at my office taped to my computer. And so on. You get the point. I strategically place them all over the place so that I can use what's called "TOMA" (Top of Mind Awareness). It's basically a reminder to myself to look at the creed and read it to myself.

When I read my creed to myself, I do so out loud and will as much passion and conviction as possible. I sometimes have to read it a few times to have it really sink in and believe what it says. That's so important. It's not enough just reading it. You need to believe in it. Create a creed that gives you a positive feeling and desire to keep moving forward and onwards and upward. Create a creed that reminds you that you are truly the best. You are worth it. You are the best possible choice for that position. You are healthy. You are a fantastic person. And then, of course, do everything you can to make those statements in your creed come true each and every day.

Sales Habitude Warriors

International Speaker and Best selling Author Erik Swanson "Mr. Awesome's" Creed:

SWANSON'S CREED !

I am the best
I am focused
I will succeed
I believe in myself
I have the will to win
I set high expectations
I visualize my perfect future
I don't let others bring me down
I surround myself with winners
I will learn and grow everyday !

*** Would you like a copy of my Creed sent to you?
Email me your mailing address ***
info@HabitudeWarrior.com

Sales Habitude Warriors

Self-Talk

What you say to yourself is so vitally important to your success in all areas of your life including sales! The magical thing to remember is that anything you say to yourself, even if it's internal in your mind, will expand and your brain will do everything to try to accomplish the command you just gave it. So, be very cautious in the words you choose and the thoughts you have. Dr. Napoleon Hill, the author of the classic book Think and Grow Rich, followed around 500 very successful business people for years and found that there were 13 major traits or commonalities they all had in common. One of them
was the way they spoke to themselves and what their thoughts were throughout each day. They say you are what you think about all day long. I completely agree! It's time for you to build an arsenal of fantastic and leadership filled words to add to your everyday vocabulary. What are you top 10 words you say to yourself and out loud each day? Are they positive and successful building words? Or, are they debilitating words that actually bring down your daily attitude? These words, whether positive or negative words, will grow and

feed your brain and your mind and expand in either a positive or, a negative way. Let's choose positive!

SELF TALK TEST

The actual words we choose to use on a consistent basis will expand into our minds and our subconscious and ultimately determine our attitudes throughout our lives. It's time to assess the words we use.

ARE YOU USING NEGATIVE & DEBILITATING WORDS AND PHRASES SUCH AS:

I can't do it. Not now. It will never happen. It's such a struggle. Things never happen to me in a positive way. That only happens to others. They are lucky. I hate that. They are ridiculous. I never get the sale. No one ever buys from me. I would be lucky if I succeeded.

REPLACE THEM WITH POSITIVE SELF-TALK:

I can do it. I know I can do it. I've got this! If it's meant to be, it's up to me. If others can and have done it, so can I! I'm the best! I'm worth it. I'm so amazing. I'm awesome! I'm sexy! *(Sorry, I had to add that one in there. Hey, let's have fun with it!).*

I'm so good at this. I will succeed no matter what. People respond so positively to me. *(Now, continue to add to this list of positive phrases and keep going!)*

Sales Habitude Warriors

BONUS: THE ABUNDANCE THEORY

Do me a favor and reach into your pocket right now and pull out a crisp hundred dollar bill from your roll of hundreds. Did you do it? Can you do it? If you can't do that, then you're not living by the Abundance Theory. There's actually a secret society of people around the world who know this little action of this HABITUDE. And, well, now you do. In fact, we trade the bills between each other as to metaphorically 'spreading the wealth.' It's a 'mindset' in which someone should be able to ask you for a hundred dollar bill, and you always have one or two, or five on you at all times. Try it. You start shifting your mindset in the way of abundance. You start seeing things differently. You start seeing that you **CAN** afford anything you set your mind to... instead of focusing on the things you **CAN'T** afford. Does that make sense? Can you think of other areas in your life you can apply this theory to? Make a list in the 5 major areas of your life and see where your mind-set may be getting in your own way.

"Apply the HABITUDE WARRIOR Mind-Set and watch your habits and relationships change rapidly."

Brian Tracy
Best Selling Author
Speaker & Coach

Sales Habitude Warriors

John Assaraf from The Secret & Erik "Mr. Awesome" Swanson

"Sales success is an art and science that can be taught and learned. Not only is Erik an excellent sales trainer, but his methods work in the real world with real people right now! Get this book and apply what's inside and watch your sales soar!"

John Assaraf

New York Times Best Selling Author
"The Answer" and "Having it All"

Sales Habitude Warriors

Sharon Lechter, Author of her newest book
"Think & Grow Rich For Women" &
Erik "Mr. Awesome" Swanson

"Are you serious about increasing your sales? Then, read this book and follow Erik's suggestions. He is Fabulous!"

-Sharon Lechter

CPA, CGMA, Best Selling Author & Co-Author of "Outwitting the Devil", "Three Feet From Gold" and "Rich Dad, Poor Dad"

Sales Habitude Warriors

2011 CNN's Hero & Americana Awards 2012 Man of the Year Chef Bruno Serato & Erik "Mr. Awesome" Swanson

"Erik is a man who captivates attention from the public thanks to his quality of speeches. His kindness and friendship are a treasure to keep forever."

Sir 'Chef Bruno' Serato

Owner & Head Chef of The Anaheim White House Restaurant

Sales Habitude Warriors

Greg Scott Reid & Erik 'Mr. Awesome' Swanson

"Allow Erik's principles to change your life! "
Greg Scott Reid
Best Selling Author/Speaker/Filmmaker
"Three Feet From Gold", "Stickability" and
"Universal Wish" & Movie "WISH MAN"

Sales Habitude Warriors

TAKE YOUR SALES TEAM TO THE NEXT LEVEL OF SUCCESS!

THE SALES HABITUDE WARRIORS

Allow Erik Swanson to take your team to the next "Pro" level of success in sales. Bring Erik in to train your team with his custom training modules and see your team's productivity soar!

Share his book with your team as constant reminders to use the "Sales Habitude Warriors" to keep your team on track each day of their sales cycle. Managers love rewarding their teams with successful, positive, quote-style books of successful training systems.

Special Quantity Discounts:

$14.95 each

10-20 Books $12.95 each

21-99 Books $11.95 each

100-499 Books $10.95 each

500-999 Books $9.95 each

1000 + Books $7.95 each

Sales Habitude Warriors

Book Erik 'Mr. AWESOME' Swanson
to speak to your team, conference or association!
www.SpeakerErik.com
www.HabitudeWarrior.com
SpeakerRequest@HabitudeWarrior.com

ABOUT THE AUTHOR

Erik Swanson has delivered over 5000 motivational presentations at conferences and meetings worldwide. As a leading award-winning Professional Speaker, Best-Selling Author and Attitude Coach, Erik Swanson is in great demand! Speaking on average to more than 50,000 people per year, he is both versatile in his approach and effective in a wide array of training topics.

People call him "**MR. AWESOME**" and you can find him sharing stages with his friends who are some of the most talented and famous speakers and trainers of the world. Erik has shared the stage with Brian Tracy, Les Brown, Jack Canfield, John Assaraf, Sharon Lechter, four-time Olympian Ruben Gonzalez, CEO Space Berny Dohrmann, Millionaire Maker Loral Langemeier, Focus Coach Doug Grady, and even Jim Rohn back in the day. Erik is a Co-Author of the National Best-Selling book 'Universal Wish' with Greg Scott Reid & Founder of Make a Wish Foundation Frank Shankwitz, and has spoken at Harvard University to their Business and Entrepreneur's School!

"Abundance is not something we acquire. It is something we tune into."

- Wayne Dyer

www.ingramcontent.com/pod-product-compliance
Lightning Source LLC
Chambersburg PA
CBHW050105230526
45470CB00004B/1679